Human-Dog Connection

Understanding Behavior
The Human Effect

"Bailey"

Lynne Marie
Canine Behavior Specialist

Human-Dog Connection

Understanding Behavior
The Human Effect

By Lynne Marie

Published by:
All rights reserved. No part of this book may be reproduced or transmitted in any form or by any means, electronic or mechanical, including photocopying, recording or by any information storage and retrieval system, without written permission from the author,
except for the inclusion of brief quotations in a review.
Copyright © 2018 by Lynne Marie:
First Edition, 2018
Published in the United States of America
Email: HumanDogConnect@aol.com

Table of Content

Chapter 1
~~Training~~ Teaching a dog

Chapter 2
Dog Breeds
Page 14

Chapter 3
Aggressive Behavior
Page 17

Chapter 4
Guarding-Hoarding
Page 23

Chapter 5
Destructive Behavior
Page 28

Chapter 6
Barking
Page 32

Chapter 7
Potty in House
Page 35

Chapter 8
Digging
Page 37

Chapter 9
Milo-Mason
Page 39

Preface

Understanding Behavior

I have worked in at least 8 different dog fields and many dog sports, for me to be able do that I learned to understand dog behavior. Humans try to use psychology on a dog's behavior but you can't, just as you can't use it on humans.

Psychology: the scientific study of the human mind and its functions, especially those affecting behavior in a given context.

Does that make any sense to you?

Behavior is learned from our parents, friends and other adult influences we had growing up. A dog is no different, except they are first introduced to life by their dam and littermates. Once they are older the human family begins. Now if their life is in a home full of anger, they are going to be fearful and may show defensive behavior. Defensive behavior could be biting, urinating, screaming, growling etc. Any behavior that is fear based activating their defenses.

To understand a dogs behavior look at the humans behaviors in their life.

*"Dog's do not have an ego.
They behave out of love or fear."*

"You don't need a dog trainer. You need a behavior specialist for the whole family. The dog is only behaving the way it was taught."

*"Adult humans can be racist'
Children and dogs are only following their leader."*

Happy T-A-I-L

T Teach
The moment you bring the puppy/dog into your home they are learning what you teach them. What you teach them is your choice, and it will be reflected in their behavior. All behaviors puppies/dogs exhibit are learned behaviors that we have taught them. Dogs learn by patterns/routines and this goes with everything in their life. All kinds of teachings are simply repetition of words and/or actions. This is what a dog picks up on so pay attention to how you respond and what you say for a specific behavior. What are you actually teaching them?

A Avoid
Avoid, prevent and not setting your dog up for failure are pretty much the same thing. How we respond to a behavior from day one will set your pattern until you become aware of what you are doing. Until a dog understands what you expect leaving food on the table within their reach, leaving socks and shoes on the floor and covering or putting up trash cans for dogs that are prone to getting into them. Are a few examples of not setting your dog up to fail.

I Ignore
There are times when ignoring a specific behavior is more effective than trying to change it by doing or saying something. The most common example would be a puppy crying in a kennel. Understand first that this puppy has spent all its time with its littermates not alone in a silent box. Instead of fussing at them over and over, help them feel less alone. You can reduce their fear by putting a cuddle toy in there and under it a portable alarm clock to simulate a heartbeat. By getting up or yelling over and over, all you are teaching them is if they vocalize you will vocalize back. They will settle.

L Love
This is self explanatory however actions out of love instead of anger are learned without fear; it is your choice to train your dog to fear you or to love you.

"When dealing with any type of behavior always look at the whole picture not just the one incident."

Chapter 1
~~Training~~ Teaching a Dog

To understand a dog's behavior, we have to understand what part we play. First let me say that we do not train dogs. We gain a mutual understanding. I have three dogs Faylyn-Giant Schnauzer, Phoenix-Golden Retriever and Hope-Long Haired Chihuahua. None of them are what you would call formal obedience trained. Our dogs are a reflection of us and how we act. The main reflection is anger and how it affects you. Dogs that learn lessons taught out of anger will live their life in fear.

Trainers advertise all over the place that they can train your dog. I can train your dog and it will do whatever I ask them to do. It is a mutual agreement made between the two of us. The dog for awhile may do everything their human asks until that human breaks the agreement in some way. When I offered training I guaranteed my training so at any point they could come back. For the few that came back months later all were caused by something the human had done or was not doing.

My girls do pretty much what I ask them to do because we have all come to a mutual understanding. Here is an example of one. I have a doggy door so my girls are free to go in and out as they please. If they go running out barking I will listen to see if they are going to stop. I have taught them if I tap my ring on a window or whistle that means enough. If you are still barking and you hear me say leave it that means enough. If you still continue I will run out there and chase you in. It works for us. A pattern has to be set so the dog can understand what exactly you are asking of them.

Remember we do not speak dog and dogs do not speak English, so we have to bridge that gap.

Mutual understandings and agreements can only be formed once the dog understands some English words and meaning. Below are the words I teach all dogs I handle.

English Words

Formal Words: Words that have been taught must do when said only once. Do not use these words unless you are ready to follow through if need be.

"Heal"- Use when you want to walk on your left side right next to you.

"Sit"- Use anytime you want to sit.

"Stay"- Use when you want to sit stay or down stay. This only works if you limit the time and verbally release.

"Come"- Use when you want to come to you and sit down.

"Down"- Use when you want to lay down. Be it next to you or out in the yard.

note: if you are in a place with more than three people be sure to say the dogs name before asking them to do something so they are aware you are talking to them

Informal Word/s: These may be repeated as many times as you like. Especially in training and be sure to repeat the word in your praise. "Good Leave It"

"Come On"-"Let's Go"- Use when you just want to walk or go somewhere. Not a formal command, so may be repeated.

"Leave It"- Use when going toward something you do not want them to have. Also can be used to get the dogs attention off anything they see.

"Watch Me"- Use when you are working with and they are watching other things (eg. Birds, leaves..etc.)

"Off"- Use when jumping on you or someone else. Also works for jumping on tables, counters..etc.

"Release"- Use this when taking the ball, stick..etc. out of mouth.

"Drop It"- Use when they have picked up something not supposed to have.

"Wait"- Use before opening the door to go outside, or whenever they need to wait but not formally stay.

"Easy"- Use when you are just walking for fun to teach them not to pull so hard. This is just for fun walks, no healing wanted.

"Bring It"-"Bring It Here"- Use when playing with a ball, stick..etc. They will come just for you take what they have and throw it or go in. Not required to sit. Just bring toy to you to play with.

How you teach these words is easy when you are consistent with words associated to action. I handled Police German Shepherds at a grooming shop and learned the German words taught. Any words can be used as long as you are consistent when teaching them. I am going to give examples of what some humans are actually teaching their dogs. I will also give examples of how I teach these words.

I will start with "Come" because this one is one that has been taught so many different meanings.

First off if the dog has never been shown what a specific word means then they will never understand what you are asking. So here is what happens.

#1a Human calls puppy to "Come" the first few time works. Then puppy starts to not pay attention to human so they repeat "Come". Human continues repeating come becoming more agitated each time. At first a puppy thinks you are playing with them in some way. Then when the human gets a hold of them they are yelling at them dragging them into the house. The energy is very different to them then what they are used to from the human. What the puppy learns is when the human yells "Come" it means run like hell because next comes them grabbing you and dragging you into the house.

#1b Human calls dog to "Come" and dog acts like it doesn't hear a thing. In reality they have no clue what the human is saying so they must not be talking to me. Even if you do say their name first, "Come" has no meaning to them. Only the related behavior you have created. Human walks out, picks the dog up and carries them into the house. What the dog learns is when owner says "Come" it means they will be coming out and picking them up to carry them into the house.

#1c Human calls dog to "Come" and dog pays no attention. Human says fine and goes back in the house. What the dog learns is come means absolutely nothing.

#1d I teach "Come" by having the dog on a retractor lead and reel them in when I say "Come". I praise and love on them and say "Good Come." Once they have some understanding I will ask them off lead. If they do not come the first time I say it. I go to him/her with a lead. I may have to follow them around (no chasing just walking) but when I do catch them I simply attach the lead and walk backward toward the spot I was standing when I first asked them. (note: I never use come with my girls I taught them "Get in the house" and if I say "Get in the house Now" it means just that or I will herd/chase you in.)

#2a Another teaching lesson dog learns. Human finds trash can dumped over and trash all over the floor and starts yelling at the dog. What the dog learns is whatever they were doing at that moment eg napping, playing.. is a bad thing. Then after time the dog learns that trash on the floor gets them yelled at even if they didn't do it. Humans say a dog knows and that is why they act guilty. They do not know unless you taught them. The only way to teach this is to catch them in the act or prevent it from happening with lidded trash cans. All they learn the other way is to fear the human coming home or into the house. and yell about something. As soon as the humans get home the dog will slink off to their kennel or bed in fear not guilt.

#2b A dog is no different then you. If they smell something that smells good they want some. Teaching a dog to stay out of a food source is possible to teach, but is a whole lot easier to avoid. This is also the same with counter surfing. Do not set the dog up to fail is how I look at it. Put the trash in a cabinet or something dog proof. Slide stuff out of reach on the counters or just don't leave tasty goodies on it.

For every word there is an action. For a dog to understand you have to show them in a loving manner. There are many things we have to do to the dog that they really do not like or have been taught not to like. When the human shows the dog that something has to be done (bath) and they will not hurt them the dog learns it is not so bad after all.

Look at what you have taught the dog so far. To change a dogs actions/reactions behavior we must examine our own actions/reactions and change accordingly.

> *"We do not speak dog and dogs do not speak English, so we have to bridge that gap. How they behave is all on the human."*

You may think you have it all figured out now that you have taught the dog some English and are working on understandings and agreements. One more thing you have to be aware of is your personal body language. Our subconscious body movements and the energy we emit under different emotional stimuli are all patterns the dog will key into even if you yourself are not aware you are doing.

Ever wonder why a dog will do something for one person but not another? Body language and emotional responses are different with each human. I use hand signals, stomp my foot, tone of voice and facial expressions that I have recently become aware of. It doesn't matter so much that you use body language and energy as long as you are consistent when teaching the dog the association between an action and an English/French/German etc.. word. **However if you are angry or frustrated the dog will feel, see and hear that and may not pay attention to what is being asked.** In return they will get frustrated because they cannot get away from you fast enough. I am sure you have all seen how your dog responds when you are happily playing with them. That is wonderful loving energy that they will respond to with equal energy.

A dog raised with a lot of negative energy will become confused and fearful. They will associate that energy with your actions and will start to anticipate what happens next. Someone who comes home angry and frustrated from work and is always fussing at the dog about something will set this pattern of behavior. They have learned that when your energy is like this nothing good will come from it and getting as far away as they can is best. They can only hope the human does not come for them.

Being conscious of your body language and energy can help you understand why your dog does what it does. Once you are aware of what you are doing you can change it and in return your dog will also change.

I used to get upset at things and would speak verbally to myself. I noticed the dog's behavior when they were around a lot of arguing. I hated the way it scared them then, now when I am upset and feel the need to verbalize it, they no longer act fearful. I learned to do it in a playful tone of voice and actually talk to my girls asking if they can believe it yada yada yada or I go somewhere away from them. There is no more running to a kennel or outside in fear. By doing it this way, I am not allowing it to change my energy, which is very obvious to dogs. You can act like you are in a different mood but you will not fool the dog, he or she will feel what you really feel through your energy and take cues from your body language.

Understanding a dog only behaves the way they have been taught, be it out of anger or love. Humans do not always see what they are really teaching the dog. See the whole picture. No dog is bad just uneducated to the human language and meaning.

"Behavior is a patterned reaction learned from love or from fear."

Kennels

A kennel, ex-pen, play pen human or dog are a human and dogs bestest friend. So many humans feel a kennel is mean, but that is if it is used for punishment not safety.

Placement and type of kennel can make a difference in the fear factor. The wire open kennels I do not recommend for an already fearful dog. Having all sides open causes the dog to have to be on alert from all sides. How calm would you feel locked in it? Covering all but the gate can help but a fiberglass kennel is already enclosed so the dog only has to watch one entrance. Placing the kennel in a corner of the room can make a fearful dog feel more comfortable because it will see anything coming from the one side and front. Think about a cave it has one way in or out. They only have to be alert on that entrance.

Playpens work wonderful for small breeds and puppies. There is only one way in and one way out from the top. For less fearful dogs an ex-pen will keep them confined and safe when you are unable to watch them. You can also place an open kennel in the pen for them to go into for more security if they feel the need. In all, the amount of space is important. The old saying for house training is "big enough for them to stand up and turn around." This is supposed to potty train them quicker because they say a dog will not sleep in its own waste. A puppy and a very fearful dog could care less about what is written. Puppies WILL have accidents (what we call it) in their kennel, ex-pen, play pen until they learn. The same applies to older adopted dogs that were never taught.

Setting up a kennel or play-pen for house training is very easy. Have something big enough where you can place a washable pee pad (hospital bed pads) on the whole bottom. You can use disposable pads, but be aware if they tear it up it is your fault not theirs and swallowing the plastic and cotton could make them ill. In the back set up a sleeping area with a bed or blanket and a stuffed animal. Dog safe stuffed animal only needs not to have any plastic parts. For very young puppies you can place a portable alarm clock under the stuffed animal to simulate a heartbeat so they do not feel all alone. Remember most puppies are raised in a litter so they are not used to being alone, they also had mom around to clean up their waste if the breeder did not. You cannot get mad at a puppy/dog for going potty in their confinement because they have not been taught differently.

Teaching a dog where to go potty starts with patterns. Take them out before you put them up. Praise like crazy when they potty outside and say nothing if they potty in their confinement. As soon as you wake up or get home take them outside and repeat the happy praise when they go and say nothing if they soiled their space. If they are loose in the house you have to keep an eye on them. If you see them about to go potty, do not scream or get upset in anyway. **Stay calm** and say something like "Wait wait you go potty outside" and carry them out to finish. If you are not watching him/her and they go potty in the house. It is your fault not theirs so take your consequences and clean it up without saying a word to the dog.

"Praise the Positive"

Kennels, ex-pens and play pens are the puppy/dog sitters for the humans when they are too busy to pay attention to what they are doing. Once a puppy/dog has learned what "potty outside" means then the kennel, ex-pen or play pen can become their personal safe place. A kennel, play pen or ex-pen is not to be used for any type of punishment only safety. If you prefer to not have a kennel set up once the dog has learned. Find a corner of a room and place a dog bed there for the dog to be able to go lay down out of the way. If you do not have an open corner, up against a wall will work. With that you can start teaching them what "Go lay down" means.

"Love and understanding makes a happy family unit."

Canine Gear

Collars:

Nylon clip may be good to hold tags but for walking a scared or unsure dog it is too easy for a dog to back out of. The clip is also made of plastic and will eventually break.

Leather collars with brass/stainless steel d ring and fastener are better than the nylon clip but a spooked dog can still slip out of it.

Martingale and choke collars are both good aids in working with your dog. People mistake the word choke to mean you have to choke the dog. It is more about the clicking of the chain that the dog associates to tightening around their neck. I used to use choke chains to work with the dogs I taught but I switched to the martingale years ago. The martingale to me is more comfortable for the dog and does have the chain section that makes a clicking sound.

Harnesses/Halters:

All harnesses give a dog permission to pull and you less control on the direction they go. Gentle leaders and other make shift harnesses will only work when the dog has it on. It is not teaching them anything but that contraption restricts them in one way or another. Think about a Horse and Carriage. The Horse has a pulling harness attached to the carriage. It is the head gear that guides the horse in which direction you would like it to go. A dog is going to go in the direction their head is pointing and a harness has zero guidance on their head.

Shock Collars:

For training shock collars are barbaric. Not only is the dog doing something out of fear of getting shocked. It also learns when it does not have the collar on. This to them has become part of the pattern to their word/action association. Bark collars only work why they are wearing them. It only teaches them not to bark when wearing it.

Pinch Collars:
Pinch collars are another piece of equipment that has many negative uses. When used only to control pulling, it can save the human some hand pain. When showing a dog in conformation you do not want them to heal. I taught all my dogs to hit the end of the lead and go. When walking outside the ring some pull really hard but that is what I asked them to do. The pinch only lessened the force of the pulling. Used any other way will only teach the dog to fear it and you.

Leads:

Leads come in nylon, chain or leather. Nylon and chain sliding through your hand can burn and cut you. Leather comes in different widths making them easier to grip and it does not cut into your hands, unless it is brand new and needs some oiling.

Retractable leads:

So many people have spoken negatively about retractable leads. It is not the leads that are the fault it is the human on the other end. When used properly these leads can be a positive aid in teaching your dog many English words and much more.

Did I forget anything? ☺

Adverse Methods?

I have to share something that happened to me on a dog forum. Someone was having an issue with the dog they rescued waking up early and scratching at their door. They explained where they adopted the dog from and that this has been going on for awhile now.

First understand this is what the dog has been taught. I can get up and carry on at their door and they will eventually get up and do exactly what I have been asking them to do since early. Their fussing on the other side of the door is just them blah blah blahing.

I suggested kenneling the dog to break this pattern. They replied that the dog will carry on in a kennel and keep them up as well. I suggested putting in the room farthest from their room and play Enya to calm the dog and cut out background noises. I also suggested they put a blower fan in their room to cut down the dogs barking and suggested they give a tasty goody when they put them in the kennel and to feed them in it to make it a wonderful place to go. This human made it sound like this dog will not settle in a kennel so I mentioned squirting with a little water from a hair color applicator. I explained to link it to saying that is enough. Mind you I understand how that might sound adverse when you know of humans that have used SPRAY bottles as a training tool to the point a dog is submissive. I received a public reprimand warning for mentioning something they considered adverse.

An individual quoted my post so I then explained that I understood how humans abuse tools in training and that I was not saying hose the dog down. That if used properly the dog does not even know where the water came from. The hair color applicator is quiet, fits in your hand and shots a single stream. The only way they would know the human did it was if they got in their face. I replied I understood how humans have used spray bottles to scare their dog into submission to the point of chasing them down with it. I then mention the 3 dogs I recently had to reprogram from being taught a spray bottle was a bad thing. Something I was not aware of until I saw their reaction when I pulled out the flea spray bottle. Not in post....These dogs could hear me spraying one of my girls in the other room and run and cower somewhere. It was not the water they feared but the bottle because they had associated the humans' anger with the sound of the sprayer engaging.

One individual debated me on all my posts saying that I was creating fear and then suggested using NILF. Nothing in Life is Free is what that stands for and to me that is an adverse method as is medicating, using choke collars, muzzles and other things recommended on that forum. NILF in action be good and do as I ask and I will feed you, do this and I will give you a treat, etc…treat reward association to everything they do……….come on no dog in my home has to do something to get a treat or their food. I replied I would never create fear in a dog, when I groomed dogs I never used a noose or muzzle. Each dog that comes into my home I watch their behavior and go forward from there. If I ever do anything that creates any form of fear response I never do it again.

I asked if this individual was familiar with a hair color applicator and again explained the dog has no clue where it came from but it happened when they were carrying on and the human said enough. I mentioned doing this to a dog recently and it only took one time. They replied again saying fear something or other. At this point I was tired of this back and forth so I said you have the choice to believe as you do as do I. I then said I was curious on how many rescue dogs they had in their home that freaked out the first night they were there. I think I hit a nerve because now the reply was not to pleasant. Second public reprimand that I saw after I had written…I would like to clarify something. All dogs that come into my home are treated the same way. Night time kennel up I talk to them telling them everything is okay and nothing is going to harm them. If they fuss I go to them saying that is enough you are fine, talking calmly. I go through all the same patterns and the above mentioned method is when I have exhausted everything else. A dog in panic mode will not hear a word said to them especially if they have a loud bark. All the drops of water, out of nowhere, does is snap them out of their frenzy so they can hear what is being said.

I then saw the second reprimand warning and replied that I understood and would never mention about pattern again. I also said that I understood that my posts would be deleted. Next afternoon I get a private reprimand in my email. I again apologized and said no excuse I just felt I had to answer posts directed at me. I then asked that all my posts in said thread be deleted. I had noticed they removed a couple where I explained more in detail no harm comes to the dog in anyway. Night comes and posts are still there. I write to forum team saying I got a third reprimand for posts I posted in said thread. I asked again for all my posts to be deleted. Posts that are a violation to your rules and I am unable to remove.

The next morning they are still there. If I was saying something so harmful that I get called out twice publically and one time privately why are they still there for all to read?

I thought I could help more people there, but it never fails there are those humans that have to debate almost everything you say. This was not the first time this individual quoted almost everything I said in a thread. This also is not the first time I have had to deal with situations similar to this. I had been on that forum, on and off for 4 years and not once did I ever get ugly with anyone but they did to me.

I will be honest; this whole situation had me ready to just give up on helping humans with their dog. This in return meant not helping dogs anymore. I spend the last 36 years of my life learning everything I could about dogs and have dealt with humans like this for the same 36 years. I was ready to chunk it all to the wind and go a different direction. No one could help me at this point it was up to me to figure out the purpose of all of this. I said okay everything happens for a reason see the whole picture. Mowing the lawn this morning it came to me to share this story with my followers. If you are looking for advice for the dogs' behavior, beware of trainers that use words or abbreviations you have to look up. Also run from the ones that bring up alpha or dominance. These trainers read books on how to train and not all dogs fit in that basket nor has a single dog read them so they do not understand. When a dog writes a book on their behavior that would be one to follow.

I removed myself from that forum and found other ways I can help the human dog connections.

Chapter 2
Dog Breeds
Hyper-Docile

Why some dogs are are more hyper active then others of the same breed?

You can look online for a specific breed and you can read about temperament, behavior, etc. The only time it can be said that all of a specific breed might be behaving the same way, is when they are younger than 6 weeks of age. From that point human interaction will either create fearful or loving behavior.

Dogs were bred for a specific purpose and it is that purpose that can produce, what is called high drive. High drive is simply the desire to do what they were produced for. Sporting breeds sports…Herding breeds herd things…Terriers ratting which includes digging…Working breeds guarding which includes barking. This is just a simple example of the breed groups. Each breed excelled in a specific activity like a retriever. A specific job bred generations on.

Those dogs will be more active in the drive department requiring physical and mental exercise.

Breeding is science when you are doing it for the betterment of the breed. The look, structure, hair type, drive and soundness are all of what you consider when breeding two dogs.

Now this is where you get major differences in a litter and why some breeds, even littermates are totally different. This difference can be from size, coat and drive (alert or sleeping).

Understanding specific dog breeds can prevent you and them a lot of headaches.

Breed Groups: Each breed is placed in a group that fits their breed purpose. These groups can tell you what type of drive a dog was bred for. When dog showing started it was a place for human's to show off their working/breeding stock. If you look at pictures of the different breeds from the past you will notice a big difference especially in coat. Now not only do you have different breeds but you also have three different types of one breed. You have lines that are bred specifically for a specific look to be shown in conformation. You also have lines that are bred specifically for high drive to do their job in the field. The last one is lines that are bred to do both. All of them can produce different drive levels in a litter and those drive levels can be affected in the way the puppies are raised. A puppy under 12 weeks of age is all about having fun no matter what breed. How and what they learn will be displayed in the behavior as they get older. What some human's forget is that a 4 month old Miniature Schnauzer bouncing around the house is cute but a Giant Schnauzer of the same age doing the same can be destructive. Or that 4 month old Labrador is so cute ripping plants out of pots but the same Labrador at a year old is no longer cute doing the same thing.

What is drive? Drive is the voice in the dogs head that is screaming to retrieve, point, chase, protect..etc. If this voice is not heard the dog will get bored and destructive just to do something. A high drive requires brain exercise as well as physical exercise, which a lot of human's miss or neglect. If you have a high drive dog and are looking for some help. Making a flirt pole to play with them with will change your life. (Pole with rope toy tied on end like fishing pole) This will work both the mind and body at the same time and not you so much. This is especially good for Working, Herding, Sight Hounds and Sporting breeds but is good for all dogs that seem what humans call hyper/destructive.

Different varieties such as Toy, Miniature and Standard Poodles as well as Miniature, Standard and Giant Schnauzers are all different from each other. There is no documentation on how the toy and miniature poodle came about. The standard and miniature are very similar but the toy is more of a lap dog then a working dog/retriever. The standards of both of these were the template for the other varieties. In schnauzers the miniature was created by breeding a standard to a smaller breed such as the Miniature Pinscher, Affenpinscher, and perhaps the Poodle or Pomeranian. The giant schnauzer had numerous breeds used in its development, including the black Great Dane, the Bouvier des Flandres, and the German Pinscher. All three of these varieties have totally different purposes to their lineage.

When looking for a dog to join your family you first have to be aware of what they were bred for. If you are looking at working breeds be sure it is not from a working line, unless you are willing to give them a job regularly. The same goes with a herding, hounds or sporting breeds. Think about how dogs do their job? Herding dogs nose butt and mouth to move herds along. Sporting dogs point and use their mouth to retrieve. Working dogs use their body weight to pull things and protect their humans or other animals. Hounds use their nose and eyes to find pray to chase. All breeds in these groups can be wonderful family members as long as they are understood.

Some of the most popular family dogs come from the Non-Sporting group. These breeds were not all bred for a specific purpose so a lot are happy being lap dogs. Again though, not all Shih-Tzus, Bichons, Poodles..etc are the same. Small terriers are also a popular choice for family members. They were bred to hunt rats and other vermin. They are alert and enjoy sparing. The way a litter is raised will also tell you if they are more doganized or humanized. Puppy mill produced puppies are more doganized then human because of lack of human contact. Show breeders that only breed a couple litters a year produce more humanized puppies because of all the handling that is required. Either way a puppy is raised it is still up to you to teach it house/family routines.

When looking for a puppy, be sure to see their parents and grandparents. By seeing the parents, mainly their dam you can see what habits the puppy might have picked up from Mom. I had a Mom that taught her puppies to bark a lot. It did not take long to redirect this behavior once puppy was away from Mom. The grandparents will show you the possible size and look your puppy will be as an adult. *note a dog can conceive on multiple days. Some breeders control the days the dog is mated others let the dogs breed as often as they want. This means that puppies can be conceived 5-7 days apart, that one they call the runt will not necessarily stay small. It is only smaller then it's littermates because it is X days younger. Again to estimate adult size, look at the puppy's grandparents.

Chapter 3
Aggressive Behavior
Aggressive Behavior is Fear

Feb 2017 I rescued a 10 month old Giant Schnauzer that was going to be put to sleep for what the vet labeled aggressive /aggressive tendencies. A dog does not behave aggressively, they behave defensively. That Veterinarian and a Veterinarian Behaviorist both told me that not all defensive behavior is fear and giving Prozac is the best thing, which had me questioning my beliefs. One night I replayed all incidents in my head of defensive behavior in all the fields I worked in and I almost had to correct myself. Pain defense behavior came to mind and it is another case of where a dog shows signs of defensive behavior. However, I went through all the pain associated defensive behavior and found that only the fearful dogs would cause the human pain. A less fearful dog will give a warning signal. An even less fearful dog will only cry in pain. A secure dog will cringe in pain or only show signs in the eyes that it is uncomfortable. A dog exhibiting aggressive/defensive behavior is from fear not anger.

Too many dogs are being labeled aggressive when it is fear based and can be remedied by changing your responses to a less frightening more positive one. There are only two conditions I am aware of where aggressive behavior is not from fear.

One is a thyroid problem; if a dog all of a sudden becomes visibly defensive it could be its thyroid. I had a male Giant Schnauzer (South) that was around 11 months old. He started showing me every tooth in his month when I asked him to do something. After too many times we had him tested and his thyroid was off, on medication he finished his Conformation Championship.

The second is rage syndrome that was mainly seen in Springer Spaniels but they have found it in other breeds. This is a condition that can act like a light switch being turned on in some dogs between the ages of 2-4 years old. I have personally seen it in Chows that were 3-4 years old. I was mauled by a Chow/Shep mix when I worked at the county Animal Shelter. This dog showed no visual signs of aggressive behavior until I stopped petting him.

I had a friend that had to have her Chow put to sleep for aggressive behavior shortly after it turned 3. I had groomed this dog since it was a puppy and it showed the same aggressive behavior toward me so I was able to warn my friend in advance.

How to lessen fear is the key to most signs of defensive behavior. This is a story of a Pit Bull, which came to the last vet clinic I worked at, for a 10-day quarantine. This guy would charge the gate like a mad dog barking and carrying on. He is going to be here for 10 days and will need to be walked outside to go potty. How do you think we should handle getting him out on lead? Catch pole? How would your own fear level adjust to seeing this pole with a loop coming at you? This would only create more fear so now what? Any kind of force will create more fear.

*"When you try to force anything,
Whatever it is will fight back."*

How I handled his fear was very simple. When he charged the gate at me I jumped to the other side laughing saying oh you are going to get me. His response was to jump at me; I jumped back to the other side continuing to laugh. I continued to do this making it a game between him and I. After a short period of time he calmed down enough that I opened the gate and he willing allowed me to put an all in one lead on him. I was aware he still had fear by how tight/tense his body was. Every time I took him out I brushed against him either with my leg or my hand accidently on purpose. I did this not only to get him use to being touched, but I also got to see how he was going to respond. I did not force anything on him. As the days past he was okay with me petting him. One day he jumped up on the counter next to me to see who I was talking to and was great with me putting my arm around him. The two girls in the room were shocked because he did not do that for anyone else.

When I was working at the Greyhound track kennel there was only one fight between two male dogs. When this happened I was the helper and the trainer was, to say it nicely, not there for the dogs. Mind you no dog got hurt. All the dogs were muzzled at all times outside of their cage. Scheduled let outs all males in one yard pen and all females in another. When the trainer disappeared, I took over and no dog fights occurred. One kennel left the muzzles on all the time. Are these dogs that aggressive? Or do they have something to fear? They had plenty to fear there from humans more concerned about $$ then their wellbeing. They spent almost their whole life in a cage. At the kennel they lived in a 4' by 4' cage. The day they raced they were taken from their kennel to the track kennel where they were placed in another kennel. They came out to race then walked back to their kennel till let out time. Not much of a loving life.

While I worked at the track I rescued 3 set for euthanasia. One older girl from the kennel I worked for had broken her leg on the track. Procedure was to euthanize right then but I talked my boss into letting me have her. Even with a broken leg she showed zero aggressive behavior. None of the dogs I rescued ever showed any aggressive behavior, two of them from other kennels did kill a cat in my yard. After that happened I decided to have those two euthanized, because it is hard to teach a dog not to chase and kill when that is what they have been taught to do. It is even harder when cats ran free in the area. Using live bait to teach them was against the law in the state but the bordering state had no laws. A dog taught to chase, catch and kill will learn this behavior very easy. These dogs are not exhibiting aggressive behavior, just doing what they had been taught by humans all their life to do. Greyhounds taught with toy stuffed animals, as law states, and not allowed to tear it up would not behave the same way.

This is different than humans teaching dogs to fight each other, most commonly known as pit bull fighting. Controlled dog fights are a sport humans came up with to make money. The dogs are taught to fight other dogs and some fight to the death. Fear of the humans caring for them is what these dogs are motivated by. In my previous book "Behind the Doggy Door" I tell a couple stories of dog fighting. In dog fighting culling of submissive dogs is common practice like culling of low drive/slower running dogs in Greyhound racing is.

Teaching a dog to chase a rabbit and kill it, is also different then a dog being taught to chase bad guys. Police dogs are taught word association to a specific action. As long as they are taught in a positive manner they will never attack anything without being told. A dog living in fear of humans is unpredictable.

"Dogs are only aware of the life they live."

When I was working at the county shelter a beautiful 1 ½ year old black German Shepherd (Magic) was surrendered by a man with his son. They had just sold her last puppy and they had enough. This girl was running on pure fear. She would not let anyone in her kennel but she was in the run alone. I have always been drawn to dogs with this type of behavior. I talked my boss into letting me have her after her hold time was up. Only a friend and I could go into her run without severe fearful behavior. Her behavior was just an example of the life she had lived and what she learned from the humans in it. The picture became clearer many months later when she was loose in our new home with the other dogs. A friend came over in his military uniform and Magic went off. She had not shown any fearful behavior in some time. She had met him before in civilian clothes so once he started talking she went up to him. You see the whole picture? She learned from our friend, the uniform did not mean pain of any sort. Association pattern reset.

Vet clinics and grooming shops are places a dog is labeled aggressive. There was not a dog that I could not handle at any place I worked. One female Maltese type dog at the internal medicine specialty clinic was so scared everyone had a hard time with her. She would snap at them when they tried to touch her. The thing was you had rounds to do every 4-6 hours depending on the dogs' condition. How am I going to do anything with her behaving aggressively/defensively? A towel in the kennel for them to lie on was not just for them but for me too. A fearful dog will snap at your hand and if they get you the injury will reflect their fear level. Putting my hand under the towel is less threatening then reaching for them and it protects my hand from getting bit. It also teaches the dog that biting is not going to stop me from doing what I have to do and I am not afraid of you. A fearful dog being handled by a fearful human is a disaster waiting to happen. Back to the little sick girl that I had no fearful behavior exhibited. One Sunday doing rounds I noticed her heart beat was off. It scared me and one of the vets was on call for emergencies only. I went and got the EKG machine to make sure incase I did need to call the vet. She was in a bottom kennel so I sat inside and hooked the leads to her as I told her what I was doing and she did not flinch. By telling her what I was doing and why I was doing it kept her calm. It was not the words but the energy behind explaining in a loving manner. Got the test done and results required call to vet. Vet could not believe I did it all by myself.

I cannot tell you how many dogs I groomed over the years that were labeled aggressive by other shops. I have plenty of stories of these labeled aggressive dogs and how they learned I meant them no harm. I do not ever use a noose or a muzzle when handling all dogs. These same dogs behaved positively when brought in for their grooms after their first visit with me. Their humans could not believe how happy they were to see me. At the last shop I worked at, the dogs taught me so much more about aggressive/defensive behavior. I was doing a hand scaling on an older, timid poodle's teeth. He had pretty good teeth for being old just tartar build up. I had him lying in my lap and got one side finished and he had done great. While I had my hands in his mouth my cell phone informed me of a received message. I figured I would check it before I turned him to the other side. I read it and replied then picked him up to put him on the opposite knee. He started freaking out, screaming like I was killing him. I thought he might be having a seizure so I held him close for a bit. He calmed down some so I set him in my lap and went to moved him. He was not having it and locked down on my hand with his teeth. My other hand was holding him up so I had no clue what to do. I slightly pulled my hand and he released and latched on again. His ears were the only thing I could grab so I got both of ears in my left hand and pulled his head back, he released my hand. I still had the other side to do so I had to figure something out. I got him to lie back the way he originally was and I just turned his head. That was a success and he had all pearly whites.

I went home that night thinking about what I did to cause that to happen. I thought of some other cases where employees have been bit so unexpectedly by fear biters and what did they do that caused it to happen. One thing came to mind for all cases. They all, including myself, took our attention off the dog. You would not think it would have such an effect on them. This is what came to me. Think of two separate balls of light, one being the dog the other the human. As the human talks to the dog and begins to connect to their ball they become calmer. That is of course if the human is calm. These two balls are becoming one, until the human is distracted in some way. In that instant the balls spring back to being two. That fearful dog has just had a jolt back to their fearful energy. Then comes your hand toward them that doesn't have the same energy as it did before. Once the human brings their self back to the dog, they can move forward calmly.

A dog's behavior reflects the energy they are receiving from their human/s. Anger/negative energy is air born and can cause them to do what they can to stay out of reach of it. Hand contact is much stronger energy transfer. When we touch them with our own fear/anger/negative energy, that energy transfer can be like a defibrillator feeling to them. They will act out however they can to not have that feeling again. When touching out of love that energy is like the most calming massage you ever had, to them. Loving energy is the energy they know how to continually go back to as their norm. The next time the dog does something humans label as aggressive, think about what you did to cause that reaction.

One day an older Spitz male came in partially shaved. He had been to 2 different shops and rejected after they labeled him aggressive. Wearing just a fitted leather glove, no noose and no muzzle I got him fully groomed. The shop owner videotaped this to show the owner how he did. He did bite the gloved hand but learned I was not going to hurt him and his fearful behavior lessened.

Bailey the 10 month old I spoke of earlier. I had been grooming her from her first puppy groom till I rescued her. I noticed her behavior was changing each time I groomed her. She was trying to bite when I would hold her foot and such. I told her to stop and held her foot until she stopped. She was not biting hard just letting me know she was afraid. I let the owners be aware and also gave suggestions on how to change her behavior. The day I got the call from Baileys human she was calling to cancel me going out to help them telling me they decided to have her put down. That was when I found out the vet never ran a thyroid test as I had recommended her ask be done. The vet prescribed

Prozac instead saying she was too young for thyroid issues and when nothing changed in a couple days recommended she be put to sleep due to her aggressive behavior. (The Giant "South" mentioned was under a year of age when diagnosed with thyroid issues.) The first time I took her out and she spotted a child she hit the end of the lead carrying on. It did not matter if they were male or female, her behavior was the same. I noticed she did not just bark at them but snap her teeth together. Her behavior was different with adults. She barked at them but not as intense and no teeth snapping. I will not share her past family's story but I will say her behavior was taught and then reinforced. Days after I rescued her with small amounts of socialization and walks at home Bailey was best friends with a friends grandkids at work. You imagine being reprimanded every time you defended yourself. You would become more defensive or so submissive you do nothing.

How puppies behave and how you handle the behavior is the beginning of their life lessons. When raised/handled with fear/anger a pattern is taught to fear having anything done to them. A puppy will freak out and may try to bite the first time they are groomed or given shots. How the humans in their family feel about leaving them to be groomed or watching them get shots can be reflected in their behavior. You are going to say almost all puppies are aggressive? No, you will say they have fear of the unknown. How you react to their behavior will either increase/validate their fear or teach them there is nothing to fear. Humans find it cute when a puppy growls and acts tough. They laugh at them telling them how tough they are. By encouraging it you are teaching them the behavior is good. Puppy gets older and now this behavior is no longer cute but becoming human labeled aggressive. Puppies will bite playing. How you handle it will either create fear or understanding. Dogs are mouthy, meaning use their mouths for a job. Teaching "Easy" instead of "No Bite" is more understandable.

Others will argue there is cases of dog attacks that were unprovoked which proves dogs are behaving aggressively not defensively. Definition of Provoked: (of an attack, or a display of aggression or emotion) not caused by anything done or said. Something had to be done or said in one way or another that triggered the dogs' defensive behavior. Dogs are taught by patterns and as long as the pattern stays the same they will behave the same way. An example someone asked me about was a dog jumping a fence and killing the boy next door. Nothing provoked the dog to do this? What is the dog's history with that boy or another boy around the same age? How do the dogs' humans feel about that boy or a boy around the same age? I would bet that either that boy or another tormented that dog somehow. What humans do not understand is by yelling, smacking (over reacting) the puppy/dog for nipping a child defending themselves. You are teaching them that child means over reactive behavior from the humans. Fear children and make sure they come nowhere near you and if they do defend yourself by all means. A dog does not attack without a reason. In the wild wolves only kill for survival. Kill for food and fight off any threats. Humans may have domesticated dogs but their survival instinct is the same.

Hitting, yelling, screaming, medicating etc. are humans reactions to their own fear. This behavior from the human validates their fear and a dog only knows of one way to respond to it. Get loose anyway they can and get as far away from it as possible. This self-preserving action on their part gets them labeled aggressive. You created this fear defensive behavior and you are the one fueling it to continue. An insecure dog will behave in fear, you can reduce it by praising everything they do you label as good behavior. Dogs love to be told that they are a good boy or good girl, just like humans. They can feel the loving energy coming from you. You build a positive connection energetically making them more confidant of themself. This connection also applies to negative energy and increasing fear level. Praise for everything they do positive even if they have been doing it for year. It also reinforces their behavior as being well learned and you are happy.

"Unconditional Love has no fear. Spread love not fear."

Chapter 4
Guarding-Hoarding

Why do dogs guard food, toys, other dogs and humans?

Food:

Guarding their food is fear of another animal taking it. Puppies in large litters begin their life having to fight for food at times. When puppies are being weaned they are fed gruel in a large pan together. So many factors come into play that can create fear of not getting any. This learned behavior comes with them into their new family home. I recommend all new dogs that come into the home, be kenneled as soon as they walk into the door. This gives them time to learn some of the new sites and sounds. If there are other dogs in the home, the kennel prevents any fearful fights until they learn to eat together without fear. Homes have the energy of the humans that live in it. Dogs pick up on these energies and that is why all dogs are emotional service dogs.

Denying food from a dog is not like taking food away from a child. Do not punish the behavior teach them they have nothing to fear. Feeding them in a kennel with the gate closed food at gate to start. Walk by the kennel to see what they do. If they act defensive don't say anything just walk away. After they have been fed that way for a few days then feed with the gate just pushed close. Teach them how to hit the gate to open it. Bailey was a hoot teaching this, I was knelt down in front of her kennel. I acted like I was hitting the gate with my hand swing down to hit the floor. She looked at me did the same as I did with her paw and opened the gate. She was so surprised the first time. I fed her like that for awhile then I started feeding her in her kennel food in the back gate open. After that she was fed out with the other girls. Each one has their own spot in the kitchen. Kennels are a great tool to assist humans in lessening the dogs fear.

Mason the adult male Weimaranar guarded his food and toys. He had been to a training kennel prior to coming to me. I do not pay much attention to it they will learn. This story was the first time he growled at me reaching for his bowl.

May 2018
I have seen what happens when a dog eats a small amount of sunflower seeds. I enjoy eating them and my girls have gotten a hold of my bags a few times. All that happened than was they came out the same way they went in whole in their poop.

This time I got to experience what happens when a dog eats a lot of bird seed. I feed the wild birds in my front yard. A while back a mouse got into the seed so I now keep it in a plastic container with lid. The girls do not mess with it so I have never had to be sure it was latched well. One day I put seed out and when I came in the lid was off and Mason was chowing down on it. I told him to leave it and put the lid back on it. Later I came in the room and I caught Mason flipping the lid with his nose. Said leave it and latched on both sides.

That is not the end of the story though. I had no clue how much he had eaten but I could see he was uncomfortable by the way he would lie down. I have a clue now, 4 large vomits full of seed in the house. When I said his name after he vomited hoping to prevent him from eating it he growled at me but did not try to eat it. I said it was okay no big deal and cleaned it up. I gave him a tablespoon of Vaseline to help what might still be in their pass and then fed him to see if that might settle his tummy. Nope, 2 more vomits food with seed, more seed then food. Gave him a little more food and walked him around outside then sit for a bit petting/massaging him, including his tummy. Go back in house put tether on him so I can watch him, massaged him more. When I stopped he did a weird stretch and I took him out back immediately He walked around and looked fine he wanted back in. I hooked him back up and we came in but I had a feeling I needed to take him back out front. 2 more vomits with more food then seed this time. Bring him and put him in his run so I could monitor him and gave him oatmeal with a drop of peppermint. He took a couple small bites and looked at me. Then he finally lay down and slept. He woke a little later went to his bowl, picked it up in his mouth, carried onto his bed and finished the oatmeal. He then started to play with the treat toy I put in there for him.

While he was playing with the toy, I went in the run to take the food bowl out. When I got around to it on his bed, Mason let out a growl. I said I was not going to take the toy, but fine I will leave the bowl also. He later put the toy inside his bowl and pawed at it till he flipped the bowl over on it. He then flipped the bowl with his nose revealing the toy. LOL Feeling better. I am aware he did not growl at me just so he could play with the bowl but it did not hurt anything for me to just let him be. When I let him out to go potty I removed both as he watched.

Humans had really did a number on him in his past, where food and getting sick were involved. Getting sick, is bad enough, when humans freak it scares the dog and they panic not knowing what to do. Masons behavior reflected this exact learned action reaction response. All the times he growled at me were the way he had learned to react under these situations because the human did something to warrant it. By me not reacting he will learn he has nothing to defend himself from.

> *"Dogs do not understand lack of food as being punishment for a specific behavior"*

Toys:

Toys are most of the time the same fear of it being taken way. It is the humans responsibly to control the situations. Do not let a dog take a toy away from another dog. Teaching "leave it" works in situations like that. Bailey was bad about taking toys from the others. If she got it I would take it and give it back then give Bailey a different toy. Dogs will handle all disputes with aggressive behavior. The humans in their live are in charge of foreseeing what could happen and prevent it. Giving treats that take time to eat can create fearful responsive behavior in an already fearful dog. This is another time when the kennel can help; it also makes the kennel a great place to go.

Sept 2017
I had a grooming apprentice move in with her 2 dogs. One was a male Pit bull the other was a female Cane Corso. Both were fearful dogs but the Pit was the one that guarded toys and tore them up due to his fear. If you are not going to pay close attention to a dog you are aware will guard or tear up toys. Then you have no right to get upset or be surprised when they attack another dog or destroy a toy.

I watched them when toys were involved. The Cane attacked Bailey twice while they were playing tug with a toy. However both times she was near her human on the couch. After that she was no longer allowed on the same couch as her human or play tug with Bailey. The pit was given toys he was allowed to tear up. Every time I caught him tearing up a different toy. I calmly walked to him saying "We do not tear up that toy here is the one you can" replacing toys. If either of them growled with a toy when my girls walked by, the toy was taken away and put up.

A reason a female dog may show protective behavior is after she loses a litter or had a false pregnancy. Some females gather toys to take the place of the puppies she lost. Her defensive behavior is out of protection. I have been around both types and I just allowed her to have her substitute litter and showed her I will handle them. I talked calm and acted like they were alive and I needed to move one closer to her. This behavior will not last long if you don't make it a big deal.

Not only female's hoard toys males will do it also. Some males as well as females hoard toys, treats, usually hiding the loot so that no other dog or human can get them. This behavior is learned by either having stuff taken away by humans and other dogs or by not being allowed to play with stuff in their past. To change this pattern of behavior I put toys in a basket that the dog can reach into. If you find a hoard of toys under a bed, behind a couch etc put a toy box near that spot. When the dog has taken most of the toys out, collect them up and put back into box.

This new pattern will teach them that their toys will always be in the box until they take them out. I use a laundry basket for my girl's toys. When too many are lying around the house, I pick them up and put them back into basket. They never have to go looking for where a specific toy is because they are aware to go to their toy box.

Other dogs and humans:

Humans call it jealousy when a dog goes after another dog when they are with the human. This behavior of protection comes from many things. How the human responds will either reinforce it or change it.

Dogs in the same house learn off each other. The mistake most families make is to take littermates, young dogs and rescues out together every time. I have raised litters of puppies for the conformation show ring. They were raised being taken out separate on lead almost daily. None of my dogs ever cared if another dog was there or not. Humans have come up with a name for the behavior of littermates being raised together. "Littermate Syndrome" I cannot help but burst out laughing at that one. Humans feel the need to put a label on a behavior associated with one factor "Littermates."

It is not "Littermate Syndrome," it is humans making up something they can blame other than themselves for the dog's behavior. They are so cute and cuddly when they are young doing everything together. You teach them they have to do everything together so when they are older they will get into things together. One reason humans get littermates is so they will never be alone. They have each other when the humans are not around and are usually kenneled together. They basically raise themselves learning how to behave from each other. Can you see why they behave the way they do?

Most of the time, the one that guards, is the one that throws a fit when they are separated. That one has become so dependent on the other to feel secure they do not know how to behave without them.

> *"A dog that lacks confidence will have increased fear and will protect what or where makes them feel safe."*

When it comes to humans it is the same. Some humans baby a puppy. They carry it around all the time only set on ground to go potty. The puppy learns this is what life is and fears anything different. Another human reaches to take them away from the one that coddles them and they will react in a fearful manner if they are not use to that pattern. If the human coddler feels any negative feeling while the other human is reaching for the puppy/dog, they will sense this and react defensively. If the humans find it funny and antagonize them, they will continue to behave defensively. Look at what you are actually teaching them when you choose to behave a specific way. You set all the patterns of behavior the puppy learns to react to.

Another reason a dog may guard another dog or human is illness. Dogs sense all kinds of changes in other dogs and humans. Any change in their vital signs will be felt and the dog will do what they can to ease these signs. When a dog's behavior becomes protective of another dog or a human check their health. Many woman notices a dogs behavior change when they are pregnant but fail to put 2 and 2 together. Now the dog is not only in tune with your vitals but also the babies. Any stress to either will be felt by the dog and they will guard them from any more.

One of the biggest reasons a dog's behavior changes out of blue, for no reason (humans think) something has changed. Animals and children under 2 are very sensitive to pattern changes. When a client comes to me saying their dog started doing _____ and it hasn't done that since it was a puppy. The first thing you do is make a timeline. When was the first time you noticed this behavior change? What was going on at that time? What changed in the family system at that time? Did you change laundry detergent? Think of the biggest all the way to the smallest of changes that happened when you first notice this specific behavior.

Once you figure out the cause/root you can than work with them to change the behavior. A lot of dogs, even cats, behavior changes one way or another when someone moves out. Think about all the energy that is going around while this person is moving out. We are not the only ones feeling it.

If behavior change is because someone moved out, that was a big part of their life. Start spending a specific amount of time with the dog, at the same time each day. You will be replacing the old pattern with the other person with a new pattern with you. It doesn't have to be long period's time as long as you do the same thing every day. All animals know when it is feeding time (if you feed meals and free feed). This is a pattern you have set for the household.

A dog that never guarded or hoarded anything before starts exhibiting this behavior. Look at the whole picture from when you first noticed this behavior to figure out the why.

Chapter 5
Destructiveness
Fearful Frustration-Boredom-Taught

Why do puppies/dogs tear things up?

Two of the main reasons a puppy/dog tears something up, excluding teething, is out of frustration or boredom.

Consistency in words and patterns you use when teaching an association between specific words for a specific behavioral response is important. Too many humans use the word "No" for many different actions a dog performs. I say "No" to you what do you say? "No, what?" correct? If you must say "No" follow it with an action. "No, leave it", "No, don't tear that up" whatever action they are performing at that time.

If you were told only "No" to everything you did, how would you behave? You are teaching word association to an action but only using one word. Next humans find things torn up and come to the dog yelling. The dog at the time was sleeping, eating, playing with a toy or very happy to see the human. Now whatever they were doing at the time, they associate with being yelled at. Can you see how that could create frustration? What the dog tears up while you are not watching it is on you for not teaching them different or keeping it out of reach.

Another perfect example is "Come" (I personally never use) and how frustrating it can be when the humans emotions are felt and their actions are not expected. A puppy has no idea what that word means. That is something they are going to learn from you. First few times used puppy might come but then they are busy playing. Human repeats the word over and over and each time is getting angry or frustrated. This energy is felt by the puppy and they are not sure how to respond to it. They come and when reached for they bolt away. They usually start by behaving in a playful manner until the human yells at them. Puppy-I am starting to see a pattern. Human says "Come" and when I go to them they are angry and do something bad to me. Would you go to someone calling you being aware that they might do something negative to you? Hence the frustration, humans are supposed to be awesome cool creatures the puppy desires to learn and be loved by.

A dog that has already learned a specific pattern associated with the word will always have the same reaction until taught different. In formal obedience for competition the dog is taught to come when called and sit in front of the human. When asked to heal the dog will then turn around and sit on the humans left side. How many families require a dog to do that? The dogs in my home are taught the phrase "Get in the house "or "Come on" (follow me) words I chose for a specific behavior reaction. Retractable leads are awesome for teaching a dog what "Get in the house, let's go or come on" means. Do not ever force them to do something unless you want them to fear you. There are infinite numbers of ways to teach word action association without force. There is big difference between behaving out of fear and behaving out of understanding.

Fear, frustration and boredom will all prevent a dog from being able to relax and rest. Think about yourself when you are fearful, frustrated or bored you are tense and look for an outlet. The dog is no different except they sometimes use their teeth to sooth this energy. I would like you to imagine yourself overly frustrated. In the past, when I got frustrated with clients, I would wait till I was alone and tighten every muscle in my body, stomp my feat, shake my fists and let out a big uhhhh. Feel better now..LOL A dog will find their own way to relieve this same built up energy unless you help them.

Exercise and consistency are the keys here. Not only physical exercise but brain exercise as well and being consistent when teaching them different behavior responses. Giving them activities to work out their frustration/boredom or items they are allowed to tear up. The degree of fear, frustration and boredom will be reflected in what and how a dog destroys something. Stuffed animals especially ones that make a noise will be the dog's favorite thing to tear up. They are determined to get that noise out of that thing. Bailey will sometimes de-squeak a toy. I just get the squeaker and repair if needed.

A dog living in fear has to stay busy. Brain toys and indestructible chew toys are awesome tools to help the human help the dog rid themselves of that energy. There are different brain toys on the market. That the dog has to figure out how to get the goody out of and can be chewed on. These toys help build confidence out of understanding. If the dog becomes frustrated they can chew on same toy. Once the dog really understands it, then it is time to get a different one. LOL... Brain toys reward the dog for figuring it out, and give them an outlet when they don't.

As mentioned earlier, flirt poles are another very helpful tool to help work brain and body. I made my own out of a wooden dowel, paracord and an octopus dog toy. Always remember to never pull toward your face when playing with the dog. Play with dog and learn how they play/hunt. Make a big deal when they catch it. By doing this you are teaching the dog about positive energy. Positive energy builds confidence lessening their fear level.

Another helpful play tool is hanging a toy on a tree limb with paracord or heavy duty spring. I use rope toy or a tennis ball because they are harder to tear up. Play with them a few times with it and they will start to play with it on their own when they feel the need to release pent up energy or just have some positive fun.

Lack of confidence comes from not being able to understand.
How confident can you be when you are being yelled at all the time even when sleeping? The human says something one time and something different another. One human lets them do something and the other yells at them. The list goes on.

"Are your reactions teaching positive behavior or negative confused behavior?"

Other then frustration and boredom some dogs are taught to tear things up as a puppy by the humans in their life. Humans make the mistake of teaching a puppy that tearing up things is cute and makes them laugh. As this puppy gets larger, this taught behavior becomes very destructive. The human is no longer laughing but is now punishing this behavior by yelling, hitting, kenneling…..Now the puppy/dog is really confused and will continue to tear things up and run from the human when confronted.

Think about how fast this puppy learned how to make you laugh. Laughter is happy loving energy. Change the way you respond to a specific behavior change the behavior. When you make learning fun the dog will learn very quickly.

When you find them with something that is not theirs switch it with something they are allowed to tear up. Go to them calmly and calmly take what they have saying "mine, you leave it" and give them their toy. I say "This is yours" when handing them their toy. You must stay calm because you cannot fool a dog, they know you better then you know yourself. Start feeling disappointment not anger, angry energy effects all ages yet the individual behavior may differ. I noticed dogs respond differently to disappointment energy.

Their behavior is like begging to be forgiven. I do not let them off the hook that fast though. I make them stay away from me so they understand the pattern association. Tearing up my things is unacceptable behavior. Set your pattern of responses to specific behaviors and stick to it. That is the only way they can learn what you are asking of them.

Patterns are how we all learn. Dogs learn all the humans close to them on all levels, including energy related to a specific emotional reaction. That energy related to a specific emotion and behavior is the pattern the dog learns. What humans label guilt in a dog is fearful behavior learned from the humans in their life.

If you praise them for every positive action/behavior they exhibit. It will help build a dogs confidence in understanding what you have taught them or they just do that makes you happy. When you praise them you are also emitting positive energy that the dog receives positively and it feels good. This is an energy they will desire to feel all the time. Dogs respond to all types of energy the humans around them emit.

*"You will never win a bluff with a dog.
They can read you inside and out."*

Chapter 6
Barking
Fear-Happy-On Job

There are many reasons a dog barks and if you pay attention you can learn the dog in your home. All dogs have different barks for different purposes and the amount of fear involved will increase the intensity. I can tell which dog is barking and what they are saying. One night though I heard a bark that I was not familiar with. I sat quiet so I could hear it again. It sounded like Mason, rescue Weim, but low. I snuck back to his pen for a peek. He was sound asleep LOL He was doing something in his dream. I then remembered he had done it before. The girls whine and he barks. With him I did not wake him but there are times the girls are loud, assuming scarier, I say their name once then "It is okay" over and over very calmly from the other room. Just like humans you have no clue where they are and what they might do to you when woke.

Back to why a dog barks.

Raised-Puppies learn from the dogs around them as they are growing up. Once they are in a home this reactive barking will carry on until "Taught" different. I experienced this with a litter of Chihuahuas. I did not raise the dam and boy she liked to bark at everything and her puppies learned it from her until weaned and "Taught" different.

Unknown-Just like children they alert adults that there is someone or something in the yard. How you react is what makes the difference in if they learn what is outside is harmless or not (you join in with them fussing at it). Dog: "Shut up must mean it is bad and we have to scare it away." What would or did you do when a young child screamed _____ there is something outside? Did you yell at them or did you go see and told them what it was and it is harmless? Teaching "Leave it" is the best way to teach them it is harmless and none of their business. When a dog first comes into my home and is barking at everything. I always see what it is, explain what it is then say "Leave it and Thank you." Here is where the intensity will vary between what they see as threatening or not (fear level). Being aware of each will dictate if you have to go see or if you can just say "Leave it."

Taught-Angry forceful man is harmful to them for a period in their life. New home dog is fearful of men so barks at them. However it is not all men only the ones that have angry forceful energy and there may also be a few woman that have this energy. They always say "Trust your dog" they are good energy readers. I had a friend come over one time and my girls had been around her before. I did not see it happen but she said Faylyn nipped her hand. It was not hard just a nip but still had me puzzled. It wasn't till a little later that it was revealed why. She had been drinking and still had some in her cup. I do not drink alcohol. The reason most people drink is to get away from their life or numb it and the emotions they are attempting to drown is what the dog picks up on. If there are no visual threats dog is calm enough to feel their energy. You do not teach a dog with words only. They can read every part of you and learn from it as well.

Playful- Bouncy bouncy bark bark…I would like to play because it is wonderful energy and really really fun. As puppies this is so adorable, cute, precious etc but at adult size and louder bark not so much. You see you teach a puppy how and when to play. As cute puppies you played with them jumping around, barking and being goofy. Now adult size but still a puppy this behavior no longer works. Bailey is one of ""Taught"" one way as a small puppy and then reprimanded when adult size. A dog is full height at 7 months of age, they will continue to body out till they are 18 months old. Most dogs are full grown and coated at that time. Bailey barked at humans with a play bark mixed with fear of what might happen. Now she only barks play at play time.

E-Fence lines-So many dogs bark at multiple things near their fence. You can tell the dogs that have learned this very well due to the deep path along the fence line. How do they learn something no human taught them you ask? By doing nothing is teaching them it is proper behavior, their job to watch that fence line. By yelling words at them, that you have not taught them, you are just barking along with them. Again the intensity of the barking is going to depend on if there is any fear involved. There are tons of dogs that find this very entertaining. My girls bark at the toy poodles next door through the wooden fence (originally taught from a Chihuahua). Every dog that comes here learns this from them and learns when it has been enough from me. If I am near a window I tap my ring on it or I whistle when it is enough. If that doesn't work I go to the back door and say "Leave it". Still not hearing me I go out running toward them while saying "Leave it and get in the house" herding them in never touching them. The last one only happens when a new dog is here and they haven't learned the pattern yet.

"Any barking behavior you encourage is the behavior the dog will live by until ""Taught"" different."

Bottom line on barking, If not taught when enough is enough, playtime only or "Leave it" a dog will do what it has always done. If in a kennel it is the same thing, they have not been taught it is wonderful safe place to go and relax.

Be sure to praise all the wonderful behavior the dog exhibits that reflects they understand the patterns of the family.

Note: Patterns are what all living creatures live by and learn from. Bark collars work only when the dog is wearing it; the dog learns this pattern quick. In multi dog homes a quiet dog can get shocked by another dog barking near them.

Chapter 7
Going potty in house
Fear-Taught-Illness-Change

There are different reasons a puppy/dog goes potty in the house. The obvious one is that they have not been taught different and they are left unattended to do as they please.

Myth: My puppy/dog goes in the same place over and over it has to be the smell, no it doesn't. It has become a pattern and this spot is usually out of humans view. When you fuss at them when you see them going in the house, you are teaching them it is wrong to do it in front of you. Puppy/Dog: "Now if the human doesn't see me all is good." It is the fear of being yelled at that the puppy/dog is behaving from NOT knowing better. LOL Humans love to say that to the dog…"You know better" if they knew better they would not do it. LOL It is very easy to teach a puppy/dog that they go outside to do their business. First Do Not leave them loose in a house unsupervised, whatever they do it is your fault not theirs. If you choose to get mad at someone look in a mirror.

Those are the ones that hide; you also have the ones that run as soon as a human is spotted. Sometimes they are finished and sometimes they continue while running. These are the ones that have not been taught anything about going potty outside. They have been forcefully handled hearing all these words spoken flooding them with negative uncomfortable energy. All they have to do is see that human and feel their energy and run away from it as fast as they can. Kennels are the best tools we have to help them understand where to do their business. Take out before going to bed/work then as soon as you wake or get home take them out (do not make them wait too long because they are happy to see you and may have an accident). If you feed them outside the kennel, be sure to take them out 10-20 minutes after they eat. Praise, throw a party, every time they go, this is wonderful energy they love to feel so will relate it with what they did. Patterns and positive energy

Another reason a dog may potty in the house is illness. I had 2 groom dogs here that urinated while I was doing something to them. Both dogs urinated blood and when I mentioned it to the humans they had not seen it. Urinary tract infections can cause a dog to urinate frequently or be unable to hold it. If this is not normal and nothing has changed in the household have it checked by a vet.

Note: Message from body- Urinary tract infections (UTI) - Extreme displeasure with the way things are turning out, and feeling helpless to change, any of it. Does anyone in the household feel like that? Dogs do not care about that above, it is the energy the human is sharing with the dog that is manifesting it in the dog.

What do you mean about nothing has changed. What would that have to do with it? Just like us, dogs live by patterns on physical and energy flow. Any type of change to those patterns can confuse them and will be exhibited in their behavior. These changes have nothing to do with their potty time. It could be a child goes off to college and was a big part of the dogs live. You have out of town guests staying with you. You have construction going on. You got new furniture. The list is infinite.

When you first notice the dogs potty pattern has changed (it can be either or both) think about what is different. Usually talking to them about what has changed in a loving manner helps and starting a new pattern that is done daily gives them something to look forward to. The reason talking to them helps is not the words but the energy you are sharing with them. Energy shifts with human emotions and new things make you happy (positive energy). Have you been happy with them like you are with this piece of furniture? Are they no longer allowed on it? Children leaving could be sad (negative energy) dogs do not understand sad energy. They do not like it much and do try to make it go away by loving on the human. At those times though humans push them away and such not wanting to be bothered, that is what the dog associates to that energy. Look at the whole picture when a new behavior appeared. The reason why is right there for you.

Intact males hike in the house because they can no different than a neutered one. Now an intact male used for breeding may do it to take claim if other males are around. Any dog can be taught not to go in the house the above are good excuses for humans to not take time to really teach the dog.

I had a friend's intact male Boxer staying here and at the time I was not aware Faylyn was in heat. He let me know really quickly and he also learned "Leave it" quickly when all the dogs were out with me in the yard. He was of course put in a run when I was busy.

If I can teach an intact male to leave a female in season, teaching them not to potty in the house can be done no matter what age.

*"Teach them with love and they will show you
a life of love and laughter."*

Chapter 8
Digging
Digging out

A lot of puppies/dogs dig for many different reasons. If they are a ratting breed they will dig up critters they hear underground. My Jack Russell used to bring me moles she dug up in the backyard. Mole crickets are also very common prizes for the dog. These same dogs usually have to get the squeaky out of toys. This behavior is not limited to just the ratting breeds. Any dog with a high hunting drive will do the same. Say thank you and get rid of critter.

Boredom/frustration is another reason a dog will dig. If they have nothing to play with outside they will find something. I have two toys hanging from the trees for Bailey (youngest ☺) to play with alone or with me. You could give them and teach them a specific spot they are allowed to dig in. When they get bored of just digging or used to your pattern in the yard they may decide to dig out and find new adventures. When the girls have gotten out, by accident, they stayed close to the house. I actually came home one day (ran to store close by) to find the wind had blown the door open and two of them were sitting on the front patio at the door.

With boredom/frustration play with them outside or be sure they have plenty to keep them entertained if they are going to be out there for long periods of time. Most frustrated behavior is due to the dog not understanding the human/s in their life. Stop yelling blah blah at them and teach them so they understand the words you are speaking associated with an action.

Intact males will find any way out of the yard when a bitch is in season in their vicinity. I saw my neighbor's dog leave the area following a bitch in season and never come back. The female did return home. Neutering is the easiest and healthier remedy, but they can be taught if you are aware of their associated behavior.

Fear sometimes sets dogs off in to panic modes and during one of these a dog is off in la la land. They do all kinds of things in this mode; main one being getting away from whatever is scaring them. Dogs have busted out of windows, dug out of yards and scaled high fences during thunder storms. Build their confidence, play with them with flirt pole, tether them to you while in the house and teach them they have nothing to fear. Praise everything good they do.

When a dog gets out often, instead of trying to catch them, herd them back into the house/yard saying "Go Home". Chasing is a game and it will only get you more frustrated and them more fearful. I live in area where dogs get loose. The ones I see I go out and tell them to go home, chase if I have to. Some have already learned what "Go Home" means.

If you do not catch them digging there is nothing you can do that they would relate to it. Fill the holes and go on. If you catch them do not scream and yell at them. You can say "Leave It, get in the house" or where ever you would rather they be. If they do leave it, be sure to say good boy/girl. If they do not leave it, then get a lead and go to them calmly. If the dog has learned to run by pattern, just walk calmly toward them with a lead and hook them to it. (Remember you can not fool a dog. If you are angry they will feel it and stay away from you.) Walk calmly into the house repeating "Leave It, No Digging" calmly. Now here it is your choice of the consequence/pattern for digging if they do not learn "Leave It" with just words. I had a German Shepherd that dug but stopped after I set the pattern that when she dug I brought her into the house and cut her nails (you can just tip them in case you have to repeat the next day).

Digging to eat stuff is another reason a dog will dig. I recently got some sod for my yard. The dogs thought this was so awesome with the new smells and tasty stuff in the soil. I had to pen off the areas to keep them from digging and eating the mud/dirt. Once the grass grows and the soils mix then pen can be removed but I will still watch them to teach them to leave it.

One of the hardest parts of teaching a dog is catching them in the act. If you do not catch them you don't have a behavior to associate with English words.

Chapter 9
Milo-Mason
Stories

Milo and Mason are 2 rescues that came to me from 2 different groups. I was told they were aggressive and was asked to work with them. These are their stories. Videos mentioned can be viewed on my Facebook page link at end of chapter.

"Milo"

2 year old, neutered male, English Bulldog "Milo" dropped off Mar 9th with behavior issues.

Evening/Night 1 stayed in kennel walked on tethering harness (my design will be posting when available to purchase) with a martingale collar to go potty and show him back yard. While in kennel Milo was introduced to "leave it" and "enough." I was able to see how he was reacting to my girls (2 Giant Schnauzers and a Golden retriever) walking by the kennel. By doing this you are not just keeping things safe, you are also able to observe the new guys response to so many things and respond accordingly. If the girls start barking they are also told to leave it which is not just getting them to leave it, but it is also showing the new guy you will protect him.

With Milo he was very excitable with aggressive features. His growling and carrying on was out of eagerness to see and/or play with another human or dog. With him being a stoutly bulldog he is very strong when he puts his weight behind it. So picture that hitting the end of the lead at you without that knowledge. To the average human that would be very intimidating only because he was not taught any different. Are there dogs that look like that with different intents? Yes, however all of these behaviors are the creation of the human.

Introduction to girls is on tethering harness in back yard. I have total control of Milo and verbal control of my girls. "Leave it", "Settle", "Off" and "Easy" are introduced/reinforced. When you have this many dogs you have to say their name first, no different than a room of humans. By having Milo on lead I am not only able to teach word association. I am also showing him again, that I will protect you. I could tell from watching his behavior what he had been taught and him not needing to protect himself from everything was not one. Milo and Bailey had very similar behavior when they first came here. Neither could lie down and relax. Pacing, shadowing my every movement, barking at every little noise and bugging you with a toy are just a few of their similarities. A dog that behaves like this is running on pure fear response behavior. When you examine the behavior and ask what created it, you will understand how it was taught. I am going to give a few behaviors and how I see the behavior being taught.

Bailey 10 months at time, Milo 2 years, see their age as the amount of time to be taught how to behave. Both freaked out when you reached for their collar which is an indication to me that a human grabbed their collar and jerked them. I just stood still holding the collar at same level repeating "it is all okay" to calm them down. Once calm I petted them and let go and said WOW. These dogs were not just jerked for doing something wrong at a moment. They were both grabbed and jerked while sleeping. Why would a human do that? Perhaps they just found a shoe, they left in the dogs reach, all chewed up.

The above human reaction also taught them it is bad to relax, you will get yelled at for everything you do no matter what, so be on your toes. Always being on edge like this creates a lot of frustration and built up energy from it. How do you release pent up energy? A dog also finds ways to this if you do not help them with it. For both Bailey and Milo the flirt pole (or toy hanging in tree on paracord) helps them release this energy in a positive way. Either of these will work their brain and body at the same time. Giving them things they can tear up or chew on also helps.

Milo had learned to get chased was how to respond to being asked to drop something. Bailey would respond in overreaction running in fear. Neither of them had been taught how to properly respond. How I teach what "drop it" means. I do not chase but I will follow continuing to point to the ground asking them to "drop it." If they drop it they are praised. When I get a hold of them I get whatever it is and I wipe out their mouth with my hand. LOL They do not like that so much, repeating this each time they learn the pattern of action/reaction. They will learn it so well they panic when they get tissue stuck to their tongue.

Milo learned to jump on humans and hump their leg. How much do you want to bet that as a puppy that was funny and not taught different? When humans find something funny the energy they emit feels awesome and dogs association a behavior to a feeling response. Now older and bigger not so funny and the energy now does not feel good, "if they would just let me do it, it will get better." Teaching Milo to sit and staying calm, he would receive petting, hugs and kisses.

Bailey learned to fear all humans especially really short ones with very high energy. It is not that she feared being hurt by a child. Instead she behaved as if the child got her in trouble. With this awareness she did not want them near her. How the human does this is by not defending the dog from the child in all ways. Then when they defend themselves and scare the child they get the wrath not the child. This starts in puppyhood and escalates if not changed. What I witnessed was barking at adult humans and more severely barking at a child with added snapping teeth. On lead she learned "leave it", "Enough", and was petted by both adults and children. To this day she does not fear humans but gets a bit too happy excited, off lead.

With dogs that are living by fear responses only they can snap into a panic mode that resembles a feral dog in full kill mode. This type of response was learned by negative, forceful reaction acted out in human anger. There is never a reason to act out of anger. Whatever it is, you created it, with that behavior in the first place. You get bit by a dog, what did you do that required that response? Milo and Bailey both would bite (not break skin) then get out of the way as to avoid getting hit. With me, they both learned when they bite my hand they are told easy and I will either hold your bottom jaw or gag you with the hand in their mouth.

Sound sensitivity is also on high with dogs taught by anger. All sounds no matter how low or high will warrant a reaction. Barking of course is the one reaction most common. Milo heard a noise behind him and in one bounce movement was facing the direction it came from with a bark. Bailey would run away from it barking.

You do not have to be forceful or rough when teaching them the English language. Forceful reactions on your part, creates forceful/fearful responses from them. All my dogs are never punished but they are aware of the consequence for a specific action. When they are not taught word association to action then anything you say to them you do not mean. When they do exactly as asked they do it cautiously waiting for the human's reaction. Milo and Bailey both coward when I praised them the first few times. You could see the uncertainty in their eyes and you see them relax as you tell them they did really good. Both would spook when you praised them out of the blue.

All negative behavior types have zero confidence in themselves when it comes to doing right so to speak. The flirt pole also helps build confidence if you verbally communicate their action..."Get it" and then praise. When I am building confidence I praise everything they do positive including going potty outside. It does not matter if they have done it for years, if they do something I like I praise. Praise energy feels good to both and it is that energy that they feel and want more of. The way you say it will depend on how much energy you would like to transfer to them. Give a party type praise is to introduce that wonderful energy when they do something awesome…go potty outside. Calm single praise so not to disrupt their energy to stay lying down.

All dogs feed of your energy that is created by your emotions. Both Milo and Bailey got shocked, in a good way with my reaction to their actions. When you stop acting as directed by your emotions and see what you are doing to them and everyone around you. We have all made mistakes in the past, but when it comes to another living creature, stop making any more. If a behavior does not fit in your home teach them differently with love.

Conversations I have with them. Milo really likes running under coffee table to avoid getting caught. One day he was doing this so I stood there telling him to go ahead and throw his fit. When he is done I will catch him and do whatever it is I was asking him. As I was having this conversation with him, he walked from under the table to my hand all sweet. Another time he had something in his mouth. I asked him to drop it and he avoided me and was growling and such. I was able to get what he had with him carrying on and then I put on a lead and led him to his kennel. He threw a fit so after he was in his kennel I inspected what it was he had. It turned out to be an animal spine decomposing. This was one of those triggered panic modes that they have to be snapped out of. I went to him in his kennel; I opened the gate to have a conversation with him. I told him he may not have liked my behavior but my behavior was the consequence of his behavior. I told him I would never take anything from him that he is allowed to have. What he had would have hurt him and possibly cause him to be cut open. As I was talking to him you could see him relax with a bit of a pout. They do not have to understand the words you are saying, they do understand the energy you are emitting.

Disappointment energy affects them in a less stressful way then anger does and is very effective.

I have a video of some of the positive highlights on his journey. These are all actions he took on his own as he becomes less fearful and more relaxed. First time outside sunning was on him he had the choice all along.

Almost 4 weeks from the day he arrived, 8:30 pm I went to bring Milo in for the night and found him already in his kennel..whoo hoo. ☺

There were a few lessons I learned and more he was taught. I am ending here " Follow through and be consistant on words used and specific reactions to specific actions. " That is the simplicity of teaching any living creature with love and understanding.

No matter how well taught a dog is, the human has to continue being consistant always. Milo was ready for a forever home were they will have to continue the same action/reaction responces.

"Mason"

3-4 year old, neutered, male Weimarranar "Mason" dropped off April 6th 2018 from Weimarraner Rescue with behavior issues.

They had sent him to a trainer prior to adoption. 6 weeks at kennel facility trainer, gone to adopted home and last a few days, he had to go. When he arrived at my home he had on a nylon clip collar and a metal pinch collar, I took off immediately and replaced with martingale. I was also handed, what I called bad boy belts, today they are called belly bands. I could not help but laugh and say you can take these back also. Bad boy belts/belly bands for an adult male Weimarraner cover it up instead of teaching him potty outside. First evening/night Mason would growl at me when I looked in his kennel. I told him all was okay and walked away. You can see the fear in his eyes in the first photo of his video journey in my Facebook video library. When I opened the kennel to take him out he was scared, stayed to the back, but was okay with me clipping on a lead. Same routine with Mason as with any new dog brought into my home, walked outside tethered to introduce to other dogs. My girls were more interested in Mason then he seemed to be of them. My assist, at the time, came out and he walked up to them wagging his tail. Bed time lights out he fussed loud so I went to him said that is enough and explained he was going to sleep in there no matter what. I turn on some music he could listen to and went back to bed. He whined some more lowly, I just ignored it.

Second night after taking Mason out I asked him along with hand signal to sit outside his kennel. He did not do it so I repeated but did not touch anything. I stood with my hand in the sit position in front of him and his eyes were full of fear. He finely started to sit but went all the way down cowering. I told him it was ok, I am not going to do anything to you. He sat up and I caressed him before going in his kennel.

Mason stayed in that kennel for a couple days, taken out 4 times a day on lead. I spent April 9th moving stuff around so that he could have a larger space. The kennel was too small of a space, he needed to be able to move around and stretch because he and Milo loose, as well as my 3 at the same time is asking for conflict. Milo had come a long way and kenneling him too much would have confused him. I feel everything happens for a reason and this was the best way to teach Mason a different life.

Mason still low growled at me and others that approached the run to say hi. If you were going to his run to let him out he would not growl. I had someone staying with me at the time and Mason would growl at them worse than he did towards me. I had noticed it was the way they walked. I told them to be mindful and have a positive purpose when walking towards him. We tested a couple approaches (I was hiding out of his site) and found Mason can pick up on your purposeful energy or lack of. If your mind is off somewhere else then your posture and energy reflects it. This could be taught by grabbing the dog out of the blue (to them) not looking at them or looking at them angrily. After a few times this pattern is performed, a dog picks up every part of the situation. They feel the energy, they sense the human's vitals, they see the human's posture and they hear tone of voice. Pattern set patterned response ready to go.

Third day I started tipping his nails that were way to long. The first time I had to use a clipper because he freaked when I turned on the grinder. While cutting he growled and went at my hand a couple times I just held his foot and told him to stop that I was not hurting him. On the back foot he spun toward my hand with a growl, I tapped him on the muzzle and said I am not hurting you but these very long nails can hurt you. I am doing this to help you. I used the clippers again a couple days later. He actually lay on his side and I got all 4 paws. He vocalized a little. The last couple of times I have been able to dremel/grind them with him just sitting there.

When Mason arrived I was told they were treating sores on both rear legs in the same spot and one on his tail. They told me he did not like you touching his tail at all. From what I could see by just looking they are scars at this point. The ones on his legs look like something he got in a kennel and the tail looks like a typical tail docking scar. I touched them and cleaned his ears to start getting him use to me. He growled and played the same swing around at me when I reached for his tail, but this time teeth hit my hand. The consequence Milo received for biting I repeated with Mason…hold bottom jaw with thumb inside mouth on tongue. I only had to do that a couple times and he has not swung around at me since.

When I started letting him out loose in the house (short periods monitored) and yard. He would go outside and walk around sniffing, hiking on everything, poop once or twice then go back to sniffing around. His behavior reminded me of a male used for breeding that lived at a kennel. Being placed in a kennel training program for 6 weeks did not help build his confidence. Everything around him is all new and he has to check it out as well as bark at it. Going on tether walk, in front yard for first time was exciting to say the least. Very strong boy, me being 5'1" 120 lbs a dog that size putting his whole body into it, requires a steady stance. To obtain this stance I had to grab onto my patio support beam as he pulled me out the front door. Glad I had him tethered or the lead wrapped around my hand would have dug in. For him to have gone through a 6 week training course and still pull like this tells why he had on a pinch collar. We worked on "leave it"; "easy" and it did not take long for him to stop pulling so hard with just a martingale collar.

Mason is not a real high energy dog in an active sense. He does not have a clue about playing or just chilling. His pacing is not a learned fear response like the others, more of not knowing what to do with himself. If he was raised in a breeding type facility a kennel or run could be all he was aware of.

Around April 18th I introduced Mason to the doggy door. He picked up on it really quick. Now he goes into the house when I am trying to play with him. Ugh LOL He's still really slow at sitting when asked.

April 18th (12 days from drop off) Video first time he played with hanging toy

April 20th (14 days) Video first time playing with Bailey

I had Mason on the tether in the house while I watched TV. I was working with him on going and lying down. Like most dogs when asked to lie down, he goes straight down allowing him to stand straight up quickly. Like other dogs I teach "Roll It" to have them roll onto a hip. To teach this I say "roll it" and softly push them onto one hip, then praise. I asked Mason to roll it, as soon as I reached for him he let out a big growl. I had him stay straight down for a few seconds then took him outside before bed time. This behavior is learned by being forced to do something.

April 22nd First time finding a toy in the living room and playing with it on the couch.

April 28th Milo went back to his foster mom. Mason let loose in house longer. I tethered Mason to me inside the house. I walked around doing things or just seeing what he would do. Inside he was in tune with my every movement the lead hanging down the whole time.

April 29th found in run sleeping. 4:45 pm found out Mason is a major counter surfer. He got a hold of a closed container of food thawing on the counter while I was outside. I will admit that Bailey and Faylyn (Giant Schnauzers) will get something at the edge, this was not.

How it transpired. I was sitting outside and heard the dogs scuffling and came in to see if Bailey and Mason were playing in the house. Mason was right in front of the door so I hooked him to the tether as I came in. (I wear it all day for cases like this.) As I tried to walk him outside, he was very interested with something on the rug at the door. I looked to see what it was, a plastic container lid chewed up, I didn't notice it when I came in because they are almost the same color. When I realized what it was I picked it up and asked "what is this?" I then replied with "ok" and turned to find the empty container. The empty container was not far I picked it up and instinctively hit them together. It made a crackly noise because it was all cracked and I did not expect that noise so it startled us all. I said "this was mine not yours" as I threw it away. Mason was a bit scared pulling away when I walked toward the kitchen to throw it away. The girls startled to the noise but they are used to all kinds of noises and quickly go on with their business. Bailey watched, Phoenix went to another room and Faylyn does not get involved in anything unless it involves her. All done so I took Mason with me outside and we sat for a bit, brought him in and put him in his run because I was busy and could not watch him properly.

Had Mason out after he ate while I typed this and I heard something behind me in the kitchen. I turn to see Mason walking proudly carrying 2 folded paper towels in his mouth. I instantly said "drop it", he did. I then said "leave it", he went into adjacent room. I put the paper towels back on the counter and sprinkled one with peppermint oil. I watch the kitchen without him seeing me watch. I see his nose up sniffing towards the paper towel (I have an island). I then see his head pop up as he was jumping. I said "off" along with "leave it" boy was he surprised. LOL

Mason is not a bad dog on purpose, he was never taught what is acceptable and what is not living inside a home. At the foster he did not learn it was not ok to go potty inside the house. Instead they put a band on him he could potty in. He has not gone potty in my house at all.

Masons sit is still very slow with what seems to be uncertainty waiting for a correction of some type. I do not touch dogs with this type of behavior. Instead I stand still making some eye contact, when they look around, repeating sit hand signal waiting for them to follow through. All the dogs I have handled in the past few months learned they were going to do as asked or they would stand in the same place, with me, until they do. I will even tell them "we can stand here all night until you do as asked." At no point do I ever show anger, disappointment sometimes but never anger. Dogs do not like feeling disappointment. Bailey really dislikes that feeling and will do what she can to make up with you (make the feeling stop). I continue to act disappointed for a bit and walk away avoiding contact.

I have to tell you a funny story. Mason has a learned reaction to the sound of the phone ringing. When the phone rings he comes from where ever he is to me walking or picking up the phone. I show him the phone and he sniffs it, when I say "Hello" he gives you one of those head tilt, ears perked looks. It cracked me up the first time he did it. What in the word pattern was he taught with some kind of ringing noise? What does he associate that sound to?

Facebook page video – video library.
https://www.facebook.com/HumanDogConnection/

About the Author

At the young age of 5 I knew my life would involve animals. I was raised with horses, a cat and dogs. I thought I wanted to be a veterinarian when I grew up but as I got older and being raised with many animals. I was not sure if I could be a vet. I did know I would work in the animal field.

At the age of 16, my parents divorced and my mom needed help. She said she did not care what job I got, as long as I got work. I knew I was not just going to do just anything. A friend of mine knew I wanted to work with animals and told me about a pet grooming shop that was hiring by her house.

That was my first job working with animals. Here I learned grooming, training, breeding and whelping. As the years followed, I worked at many grooming kennels and also got experience as a veterinarian technician. As a technician I worked at different clinics including emergency and specialty clinics.

Having grooming experience, I was able to get involved in dog showing. I worked for two of the top handlers in my area in the 80's. Both taught me handling and grooming skills that I was grateful to learn. I taught Grooming at a Grooming Academy and a Community College.

With my training experience, I got a job working for a few Greyhound racing kennels including one breeder kennel. It was an experience that was not anything I ever wanted to do again. With kennel and vet tech experience, I then qualified for a job at the county animal shelter where I lived. There were lots of heartaches to experience there. This was where I truly learned how evil some humans can be when it comes to their pets and how they treat them. After that I went back into a grooming/training/handling business with a partner and I got the pleasure to be head trainer of our county K-9 search and rescue team. The whole team received a certification for land search with their dog by a certified Search and Rescue Trainer/Author.

Today I can groom all fearful small, medium and some large breed dogs without a noose or muzzle just one leather glove. I can scale teeth without sedation just by laying the dog in my lap. All dog behavior is a reflection of the type of human interactions they have had. It is not about obedience but working together with compassion and love. All we are doing is teaching a foreigner the English language. How we do that is what makes a difference.

All of my knowledge/wisdom is from experience not from a book/ books I read. What I speak of and teach is simple, easy to understand information from personal experience. My long term goal is educating the masses by having speaking engagements.

Printed in Great Britain
by Amazon